I0471794

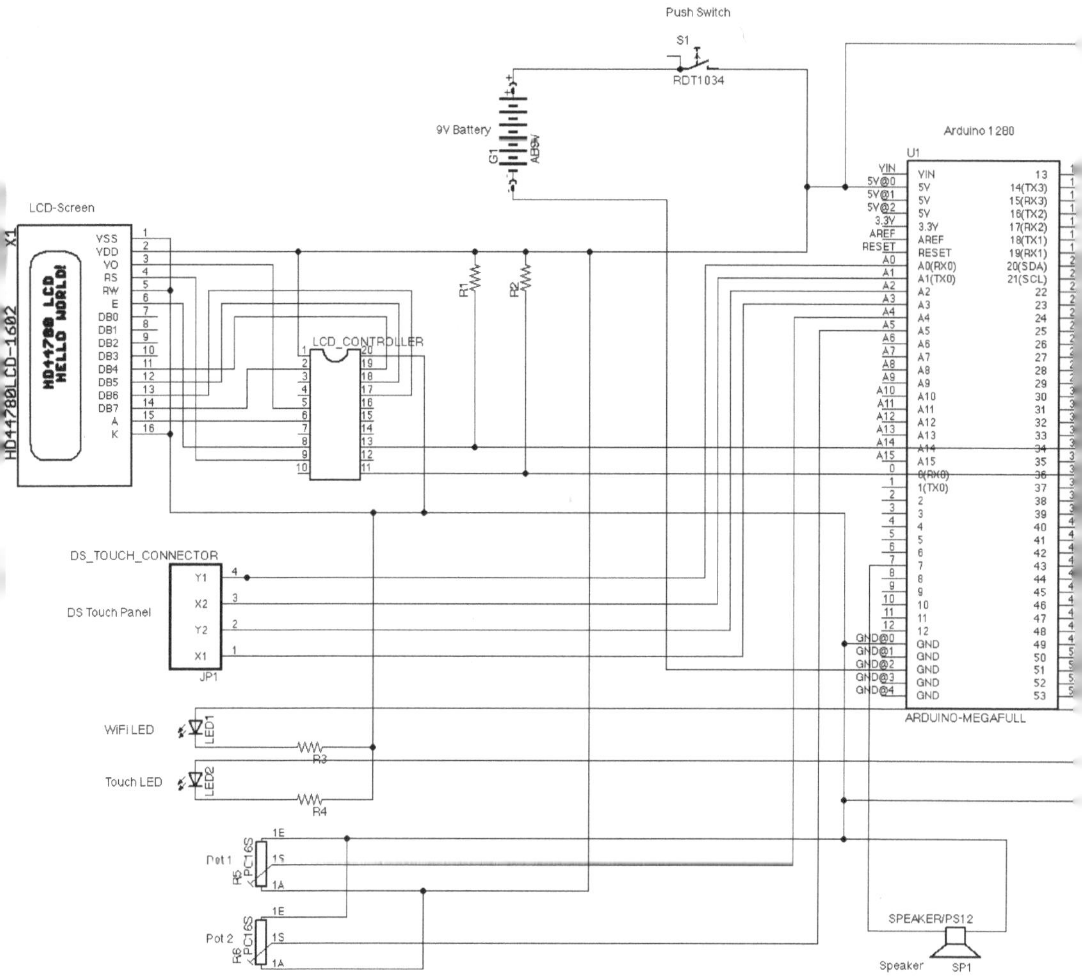

Push Switch

S1
RDT1034

9V Battery

Arduino 1280

U1

VIN	VIN	13
5V@0	5V	14(TX3)
5V@1	5V	15(RX3)
5V@2	5V	16(TX2)
3.3V	3.3V	17(RX2)
AREF	AREF	18(TX1)
RESET	RESET	19(RX1)
A0(RX0)	A0(RX0)	20(SDA)
A1	A1(TX0)	21(SCL)
A2	A2	22
A3	A3	23
A4	A4	24
A5	A5	25
A6	A6	26
A7	A7	27
A8	A8	28
A9	A9	29
A10	A10	30
A11	A11	31
A12	A12	32
A13	A13	33
A14	A14	34
A15	A15	35
0	0(RX0)	36
1	1(TX0)	37
2	2	38
3	3	39
4	4	40
5	5	41
6	6	42
7	7	43
8	8	44
9	9	45
10	10	46
11	11	47
12	12	48
GND@0	GND	49
GND@1	GND	50
GND@2	GND	51
GND@3	GND	52
GND@4	GND	53

ARDUINO-MEGAFULL

LCD-Screen

X1

HD44780LCD-1602

HD44780 LCD
HELLO WORLD!

VSS	1
VDD	2
VO	3
RS	4
RW	5
E	6
DB0	7
DB1	8
DB2	9
DB3	10
DB4	11
DB5	12
DB6	13
DB7	14
A	15
K	16

LCD_CONTROLLER

R1 R2

DS_TOUCH_CONNECTOR

DS Touch Panel

Y1	4
X2	3
Y2	2
X1	1

JP1

WiFi LED   LED1   R3

Touch LED   LED2   R4

Pot 1   R5   PIC16S   1E 1S 1A

Pot 2   R6   PIC16S   1E 1S 1A

SPEAKER/PS12

Speaker   SP1

Francesca Perona, *Digital Embroidery*, detail.

Physical Computing at Goldsmiths

Edited and introduced by
Brock Craft and Eleanor Dare

Goldsmiths
UNIVERSITY OF LONDON

Physical Computing at Goldsmiths

by Brock Craft, Eleanor Dare and contributing authors.

© 2012, some rights reserved.

Introduction

This modest, carefully composed book highlights the scope of Physical Computing at Goldsmiths, University of London. Physical Computing is a challenging and relatively new domain of practice that blends elements of electronics, computing, interaction design, and creative exploration. Tom Igoe, author and co-creator of the popular Arduino microcontroller platform describes it as "an approach to learning how humans communicate through computers that starts by considering how humans express themselves physically". We use sensors to mimic, augment, and surpass the body's own sensory capabilities, detecting changes in light, sound, temperature, pressure, and so on. These signals can be processed, interpreted, changed, and redirected according to logic programmed onto small microcontrollers, similar to the way (and faster than) the human brain can respond to sensory input. Although it has been possible to do this for decades, new tools and resources are now available at relatively low cost and are easy to use. Thus, ideal conditions have emerged for new kinds of creative exploration and expression, and new groups of practitioners are eagerly engaging with and redefining human expressive potential. The broadened scope for creative investigation is extraordinary and invigourating.

This book showcases the work of students mainly from the department of Computing at Goldsmiths who have attended the Physical Computing modules taught at the college. Each of these students has investigated first-hand the possibilities and boundaries inherent in working with the human body as a given, which requires us to "design within the limits of its expression" and within its enormous capabilities for interpreting and understanding the world. As Goldsmiths postgraduate student Samuel Price characterises it, "The very definition of Physical Computing is a vast and fascinating pursuit." Samuel strives to "interpret our analogue world through digital and physical constructs". Other students are concerned with the way in which old and new technologies might blend in exciting new forms.

The projects in this book are arranged into three broad categories of work. However, owing to the huge number of creative avenues that can be explored, it would be misguided to try to organise them according to a few, rigid characteristics of inputs, outputs, or techniques. Thus, we have arranged the projects in loosely related topical clusters, based on similarities in the areas that students have worked. The first grouping consists of investigations of the material, tactile, and dynamic. These projects have movement and physicality at their core, and most of them involve motion, audio. The second cluster of work probes environments, sensors within environments, and connectivity to networks. They comprise work that interprets environmental characteristics, responding and reacting to these, and in some cases communicating locally or to the internet. The third cluster is distinguished by the relational, the liminal, and the luminous. These explore the interstices and interactions between ourselves and others, inner spaces and moods, through the use of light and projections. Some of these integrate performative work and interactivity.

As a corpus, this collection opens an aperture into the diverse objects, spaces, and interactions that can be realised within the realm of Physical Computing. Many of the projects investigate perhaps impractical, implausible, or quirky questions and possibilities. This uncertain locus is precisely the place to be – where creative investigation can yield its highest potential. It is fruitful terrain, the birthplace of new ideas, expressions, and aspirations. Our students, our co-authors, our collaborators in these journeys have worked quite rigorously to find their expressions here and it has been a pleasure to share and learn along the way. This book showcases their work in their own words, through descriptions of their experiences working in this evolving frontier. Many have also discussed their thoughts on Physical Computing as a process, describing their objectives, challenges, and reflections about their work. We hope you will find these projects as fascinating, surprising, and inspiring as we do.

Brock Craft and Eleanor Dare
London, 2012

material

tactile

dynamic

Pixsol

Philo van Kamenade,
MSc Cognitive Computing

Cocktail umbrellas, wood, Arduino microcontroller, servo extender IC, miniature servos.

PixSol is an interactive art installation that shows the process of pixellisation in images at a human-perceivable scale. While mostly unaware of it, we often see continuous-looking images represented by miniature lights of varying intensity all around us in digital displays. PixSol makes this pervasive technique approachable by rendering the visual effect in life-size physical cocktail umbrellas.

As a kid, I discovered that these magical fabrications carry within them hidden messages in a secret language. Years later, I've figured out those messages are just bits of Chinese newspaper, but the umbrellas still manage to spark the imagination. After all, don't they just seem like the perfect object to use as adjustable pixels in a physical monitor project?

During construction, the flimsy character of the umbrellas caused some challenges, especially in the connection from the servo motors to umbrella sticks. A large scale-up of this project will have to be more modular and more precise in the actuation of the umbrellas.

They nice thing about physical computing is the many different ways of thinking it requires. There's the issue of representing your ideas in the code you're writing and at the same time there are all these

constraints to satisfy in the physical build. Combining these different ways of problem solving is a real challenge but extremely enjoyable when you see your project moving ahead!

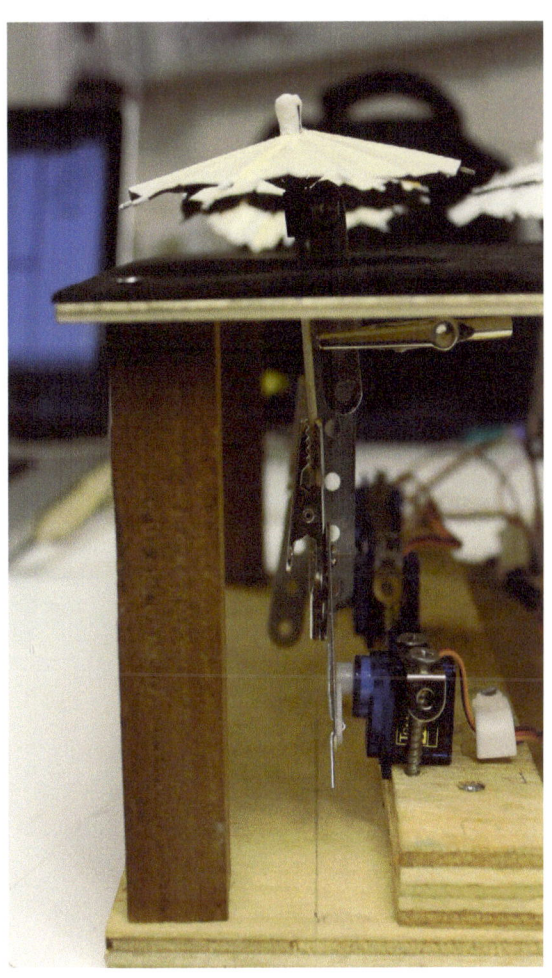

Real Drum Sequencer

Konstantin Grachev, BMus Music Computing
Zeb Pedersen, BMus Music Computing

Assorted percussive instruments, found housings, Arduino microcontroller, solenoids.

The Real Drum Sequencer brings the programmable world of electronic drum machines into the physical domain, linking electronic drum sequencing capabilities with actual percussive instruments. This project also replicates the features of a digital drum set, but substitutes prerecorded samples for real drums. We've created a genuine 100% physical drum machine, with a sequencer control unit which which connects to a series of real drums, modified with electronically controlled hammers activated by the sequencer unit.

When creating music using computers, there are two tools which are very commonplace: sequencers and samplers. Sequencers are a control mechanism that stores a pattern of notes or events and acts upon them as the program is iterated through. These events are regularly used as triggers for samplers which will, when instructed by the sequencer, play back a recording or synthesize a sound.

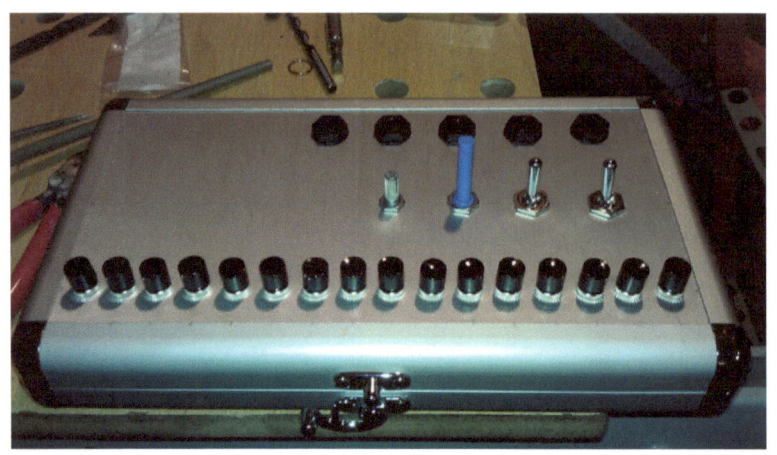

Early drum sequencers such as the Roland TR-808 Rhythm Composer contain both a sequencer and a synthesizer for generating sounds. The 16-step sequencer stores the patterns for each drum and plays through them at a user-defined tempo, synthesizing a range of drum-like sounds using its built-in analog synthesis capabilities.

Most contemporary computer musicians have abandoned expensive and sometimes unreliable dedicated hardware sequencers for entirely software based tools, such as Izotope iDrum. In our project we aimed to take a step back from the modern day software-only drum machines and return to the physical world of the 808. Furthermore, we abandoned the synthesised and sampled drum effects from our approaches.

There were two distinct challenges in this project: creating a programmable Arduino sequencer, and building a range of physical controls and actuators. The sequencer was developed initially using blinking LEDs, and was kept separate from the high-power solenoids and the drums themselves until later in the project. The

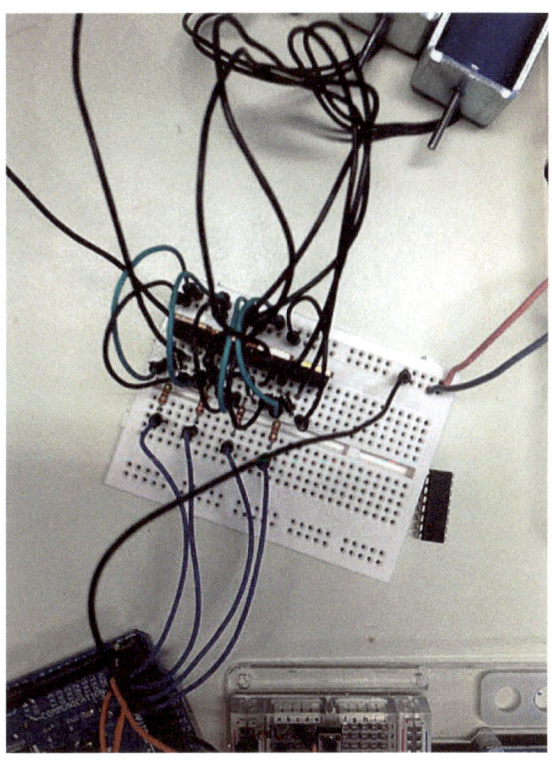

final format of the system, comprising a separate control unit and 'drum box', allows a modular approach to be taken – by simply plugging a different set of drums into the controller, many different sounds can be produced.

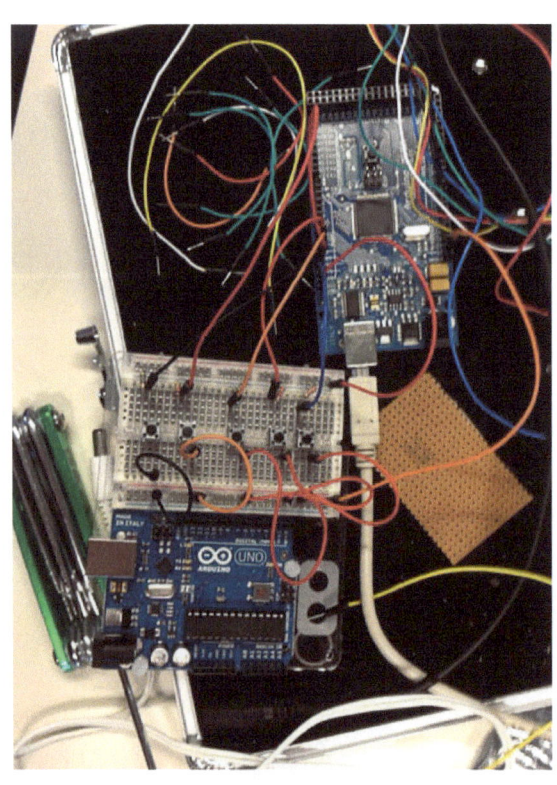

Inter-

Joowon Chung, MFA Computational Studio Arts
Deoksun Park, MA Computational Arts

Wood, Arduino microcontroller, light dependent resistors, puredata.

This project suggests different method of interplay (communication) between the audience and the work in interactive art. in general, interactive art uses visualisation as its main basis. The combinations of sound and visualization or sound and physical movements form the mainstream in this field. On the other hand, a person who is not using visual sensation as his or her main method of communication faces some difficulties in appreciating interactive art. Therefore, we have made an interactive art project for an audience who uses different senses to communicate with people. The project aims to remove barriers between people.

Although the majority of interactive art works use more than one sense, such as a combination of sound and visual cues, or sound and touch, ironically such combinations of senses are still based on visual content. Those limited aspects inspired us to start thinking about people who do not use vision as a major medium for communication.

Our project, *inter-* is aimed at creating physical output. One of our project keywords is "touchable", so we had to think about both perspectives of touch, with sighted and visually impaired people. Hence, we chose Braille, which is readable by the blind, but is not usually understood by those who use as their primary means of communication.

This object operates when the user reads and touches a wooden surface at which point, the dots of the Braille letters make sounds in relation to the movement of the users' fingers. However, this Braille is different from conventional Braille, in that the dots composing each letter are not raised, but are in fact holes. When these holes are covered with the finger, the light sensors (LDR) mounted inside detect the light variations, and send a signal to the

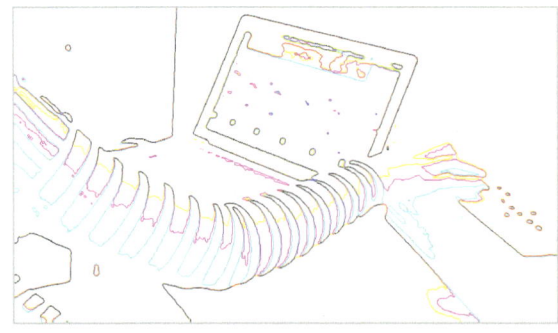

onboard microcontroller. This signal is interpreted by *puredata* software, which modulates audio accordingly. If a hole is covered, the *inter-* box will make a sound that follows the movement of a finger. By the action of a finger, people with sight can feel the sound of a letter. On the other hand, people without sight can build an auditory meaning of a word and feel the symphony of sound as well.

Through *inter-*, people can be reminded of the differences of their senses, of alternative communication methods and aesthetic experiences.

roboArm

Thibault Lelievre, MSc Cognitive Computing
Dean Spiridonov, MSc Cognitive Computing

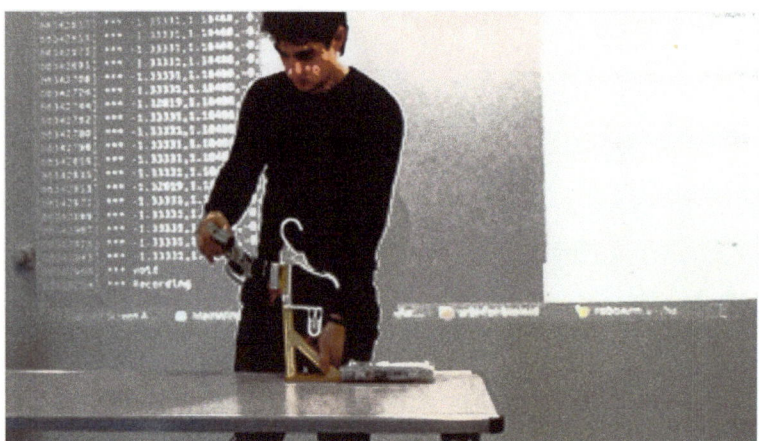

Custom servomotors, wood, found materials.
http://botarm.wikispaces.com/

The main idea of the project was to build a physical robotic arm that would mimic normal human arm movements. The robotic arm works in two different ways, which are both controlled through a custom-made user interface and implemented programmatically through two methods.

The first method records the arm's movements via embedded sensors. Manually moving the arm during the record function stores data about movements that have been executed. The recorded motions can then be replayed. A second method uses the keyboard to manually control the robotic arm.

We were motivated to develop this project because we were interested in whether it is possible to create a simple robotic arm, made out of servos, to copy human-like arm movements. During development there were a few problems encountered such as connecting Urbiscript to an external application that would allow us to send serial messages from one program

to another. This allowed the project to have a custom made user interface, enabling users to point and click on a function to be executed, or to simply use the keyboard to control the arm.

We find Physical Computing fascinating because it allows people to show their creativity and develop systems that have not been developed before, like the *roboArm*. The *roboArm* project uses physical hardware components to build the robotic arm and then have it programmed to execute functions that are designed by the user.

The project wiki website has more information about its construction, including examples and project code.

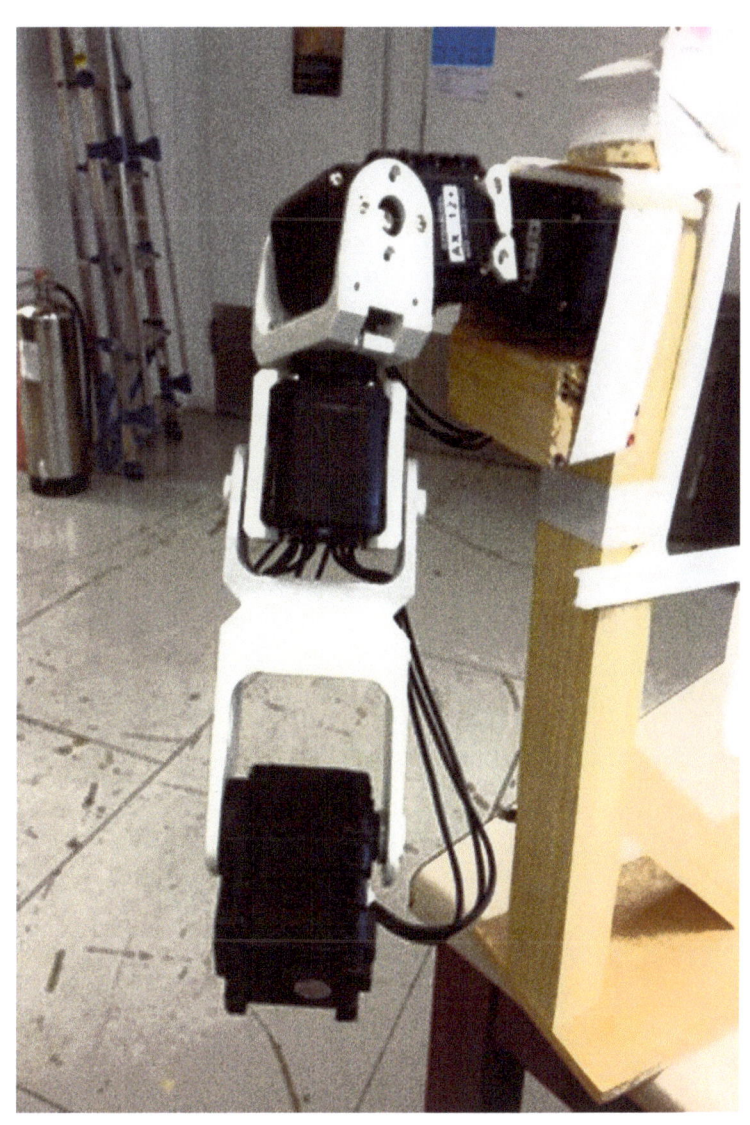

FUBox

Emil Lewandowski, BMus Music Computing
Grant McNeill, BMus Music Computing

Arduino microcontroller, deconstructed speaker, guitar pickup and strings, piezoelectric transducer.
Video: http://bit.ly/KKC5R1

Sonification and generative music have been central to our artistic endeavours since we started the Music Computing course, and we wished to extend this to Physical Computing. Thinking further about this prepared guitar, we decided it would be a fitting idea to try to sonify the *learn.gold* course forum online. This project is a reinterpretation of our studies, with the actual teachings embedded in the sound output. The sonification allows the *FUBox* to act seemingly autonomously, as it parses and interprets the course forum web page. The the text of the course content used as source material which is sonified.

Employing Pulse Width Modulation to send signals to a deconstructed speaker, we attached various matierals to the vibrating parts of the speaker in order to amplify the sound. We took apart an old guitar and used some of the components to fasten strings across a wooden soundboard and used various materials to study the

overtones produced by manipulating the frequency the speaker vibrates at.

We attached a piezoelectric element to the sound bridge in order to capture all of the overtones being produced by the strings, as well as the vibrations of the *FUBox* itself and the fundamental frequency being produced by the speaker. The result is then amplified through a guitar amp.

A servomotor attached to a piece of wire creates tension across a metal bar which rests upon the guitar strings. This servo is programmatically controlled, and allows us to change the overtones being produced by the strings. The servomotor rotates to actuate the metal bar, thereby applying different amounts of pressure upon the strings, changing the quality of the sound output.

The *FUBox* "plays" text which is read from a computer and taken from textual content related to the course, by decoding the ASCII values of the letters from the online forum. Letters are mapped to specific audio frequencies. Capital letters act as a signal to change the tension of the servomotor's wire. Playback speed can be manually controlled by an onboard potentiometer. The resulting sound is a bit chaotic, but *FuBox* is an enlightening experiment in generative computer controlled audio. Overall, we are very pleased with the outcome of our project.

Road I Nu

Nicola Blackwell, BSc Computer Science
Ben Clements, BSc Computer Science

Arduino microcontroller, XBee wireless module, joystick controller, motorised tank assembly, LEDs, light dependent resistor.

Road I Nu is a project that brings physical computing to life in a fun and retro way. The main aim for this project was to build a remote control car with both sensors and actuators. We wanted the car to have LEDs, motors, a light dependent resistor, a toggle switch, wireless communication, and a remote control. It uses a simple remote control device that utilizes an eight way joystick.

Even small projects can encounter bumps in the road, and for us it was the challenge of using wireless communication. Trying to keep things small using generic parts that are affordable means you really do need to design the project well, making sure everything fits and will work together.

The most interesting aspect of physical computing is the range of possibilities using the latest technology and the unique ways it can be applied. The only limits to overcome are those of your own creativity and inspiration.

Alarm Clock

Kenneth Read, BSc Creative Computing
Mark Woulfe, BSc Creative Computing
http://morephysicalthancomputing.tumblr.com/

Arduino microcontroller, real time clock module, audio playback shield, found housing.

Alarm Clock is simply a handmade wooden alarm clock powered by an Arduino Uno microcontroller. It consists of an LCD screen which displays the time, a real time clock with backup, so that time can be kept even if the battery dies, an audio playback module along with a small speaker to play music for the alarm, 4 buttons on the back to adjust the time, date and alarm, and a tilt sensor to sense which way up the alarm clock is. The accompanying SD card allows the user to choose their own song or noise to use as their alarm. When the alarm time is set using the buttons on the back, the alarm is armed. Once it goes off, the user can then turn the alarm clock upside down, triggering the tilt switch, which will turn off the alarm.

What we found challenging was how to fit together all the different components that we wanted to use for the clock. We had to make sure there were no clashes in hardware ports or software libraries, and to make sure the code worked to allow

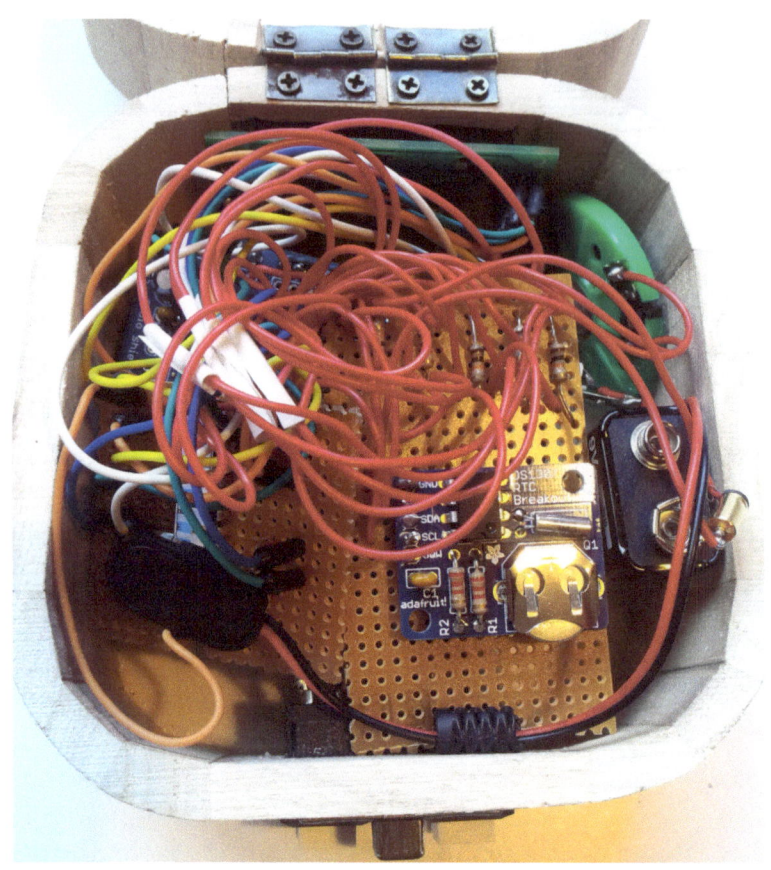

each part to function together. Getting the LCD screen to work with a display driver chip so that it only used two input pins (made necessary by a lack of available pins) was also a challenge we had to overcome.

Physical Computing was a fresh experience that allowed us to combine coding knowledge we already had with electronics. Our project was an example of how you can take an everyday object and add your own innovations to create something new and interesting.

Digital Embroidery

Francesca Perona,
MFA Computational Studio Arts
Irene Regueiro Sanchez,
Collaborating Artist

Assorted textiles, Lilypad microcontroller, shape memory alloy wire, beads, LEDs, conductive thread, springs.

Influenced by my Textile Design background, I developed an interest in e-textiles and smart materials. I am interested in cross-field experimentation, integrating computational technologies with traditional craft.

Digital Embroidery has been a first attempt in the expanded field of e-textiles. I found it engaging, challenging and time consuming. I realised that adding a computational element to fabrics requires both advanced craft skills and careful planning of the circuit.

Circuitry has been the main focus of the project in terms of computational implementation. The code is therefore straightforward, and is designed to activate the interactive dialogue between viewer and interface.

I focused on the qualities of the materials, layering the artwork and developing 3-dimensional embroidery to instigate an haptic response. I also focused on colour, taking inspiration from human circuitry: the

vascular system, and cellular conformations.

The nitinol wire I used is reminiscent of muscle contractions, reproducing organic, aesthetically subtle movements. Nanoscale and macroscale blend together on the surface, producing a behavioural tactile interface.

I tried to mediate the challenges of electronic circuitry with the fluidity of fabrics. I faced the difficulty of constructing a reliable circuit that draws enough current for good performance of the parts. The embroidery work has to be precise, but thick at the same time over considerable lengths. The connections with strip-board and other parts are tricky and there is a high risk of burning out the circuit. Threads tend and knots tend to gradually become untied through flexion, and therefore require insulation through the application of thick layers of silicone. I felt the need to work with the Lilypad microcontroller instead of Arduino, to overcome otherwise problematic connections.

Apart from the general challenges, nitinol wires are a demanding material to work with as well. While testing the circuit on reliable structures, I didn' t realise that the application to soft fabrics would be harder. I had to plan the positioning of the wires

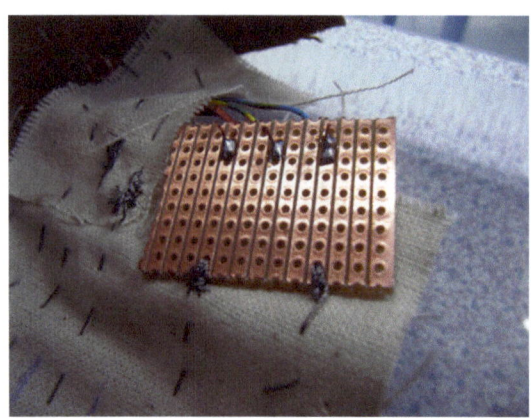

several times to achieve a decent result. As the nitinol requires considerable amounts of current to contract, I had to work with short lengths, which produced a less visible result than planned.

There are not many examples of the application of this material to the Textile field. It is worth investigating because nanotechnologies are the future. I believe this research area needs to be fully investigated both theorically and practically.

environmental

sensory

networked

Digital Brownie

Fernando Galdon, MSc Cognitive Computing
Catherine Weir, MFA Computational Studio Arts
www.cmweir.com

Arduino microcontroller, real time clock module, audio playback shield, retrofitted Brownie Camera housing.

In 1900 Kodak produced the first *Box Brownie* camera retailing for $1, including the cost of processing the film. This simple low-cost camera played a key role in introducing the medium of photography to a wider audience. Kodak continued to manufacture the *Brownie* series up until around 1980, making it arguably their most iconic camera.

At one point, around ninety per-cent of film sold in the United States was made by Kodak, but in January 2012 the company was forced to file for bankruptcy, following their failure to adapt to new consumer demands for digital cameras. This is perhaps somewhat ironic, as it was Kodak engineers who first invented the digital camera in 1975. The prototype model was roughly the size of a toaster and took twenty-three seconds to take a 0.01 mega-pixel black and white photograph.

Arguably, digital photography is in some ways the 21st century equivalent to the Box Brownie camera, making simple, low-cost photography available to a huge

audience. *Digital Brownie* is intended to combine the convenience of digital photography with the body of an old *Brownie* camera to create a unique image-making device. It uses the modified body of a Kodak Box Brownie to house a webcam connected to a computer via USB. An Arduino microcontroller detects when the user presses the shutter of the camera and sends a signal to a Processing sketch running on the computer to tell it to process the incoming data.

The images produced are partly inspired by the kind of photographs that might have been taken with Kodak's prototype digital camera; namely black and white long exposure images. Users are able to hold the shutter open, capturing a number of video frames which are processed in order to create one still image. Once the photograph has been taken the picture is displayed on the computer's monitor. Here, the user has the option to either save the image to disk or share it online through Flickr. In order to take another photograph, it is necessary to "wind-on" the camera; the existing mechanism to wind film activates a sensor which re-sets it to capture the next image.

The main body of the *Browine* camera is a purely mechanical device; it does not have any power source and everything is controlled by moving parts. In keeping with the aesthetic of the camera, we used as many of the existing mechanisms as possible. The shutter of the camera is activated by pressing a button on the front side of the camera, which moves a metal plate across the front of the lens. A

piezoelectric sensor senses when the piezo is struck by the metal plate, which send a signal to Processing to start capture of the image.

A *Brownie* has two viewfinders, located on the top and on one side of the camera, for taking either portrait or landscape images. An internal tilt switch detects when the *Digital Brownie* is held in a landscape or portrait position.

Arguably, digital photography is in some ways the 21st century equivalent the Box Brownie camera, making simple, low-cost photography available to a huge audience. This project combines the convenience of digital photography with the body of an old *Brownie* camera to create a unique image-making device. The nature of the device means that it does not create perfect digital images, but ones unique to its particular setup. The hope is that this will help to re-capture some of analog photography's charm that many regard as having been lost since the advent of digital cameras.

IR Twigs

kyriakos kousoulides, MA Computational Arts

Arduino microcontroller, twigs, infrared emitters and sensors, LEDs.

I thought it would be interesting to try to make a sculpture that combines strictly earthly and natural materials with circuits, sensors, and cables. I wanted to emphasise the contrast between the two mediums, so I used raw branches instead of industrial wood. I started collecting them in my bag whenever I found one on the street or in a park; I didn't want to cut them from the trees. Thankfully, it was autumn and you can find a lot of branches in London, if you know where to look.

The idea behind *IR Twigs* was to take something lifeless or inanimate, if you like, and give it input and output sensors and also make it communicate with other objects of its own kind – and then release it back in nature as a free...twig.

I wanted the shape of the creature to occur use functional characteristics rather than aesthetic, and I didn't want to have only one output and just change the message randomly or with a button. Rather, I wanted a message to be determined by the position of the object,

relative to the others. They would send IR messages that would affect each other. The most practical and efficient shape to send the highest possible amount of infrared beams is a triangle or a prism. In order to have messages sent from each corner, I decided to use three infrared sensor beams on each corner, the centre of each, I put a receiver. Each message/corner represents one colour (RGB) and by rotating one object your would change the colour of the other.

Since we had 3 inputs, 3 outputs, and 3 colours, I decided to create 3 creatures. Physical Computing was a fresh experience that allowed us to combine coding knowledge we already had with electronics. Our project was an example of how you can take an everyday object and add your own innovations to it to create something new and interesting.

Dynamic Spaces

Jonathan Munro
MFA Computational Studio Arts
www.jonathanmunro.com

Wood, LEDs Arduino microcontroller, servo motors, proximity sensors.

Dynamic Spaces is a mock-up for plans to create a full scale installation, with two walls which open and close depending on the position of the audience in the middle. The installation is aimed to provide two different forms of audience engagement. One is for people who walk into the centre of the two walls, then experience the walls closing off the exit. The second is for those who can walk around the two walls, experiencing a different shift in space around the room. As the walls close, if the audience is too close them they may be forced to move in accordance, shifting with the internal and external dimensions within a corridor.

One of the technical issues I experienced was in getting two stepper motors to rotate at the same time and distance. I used a motor shield which allowed me to use a couple of external libraries, but this still proved to be a challenge. Following this development I decided to take the project in a different direction than originally planned. The walls became more un-

predictable in their movement and instead of them mirroring each other's movement, I found it more interesting to see what would happen if they moved by different amounts. The audience are left with a motivation to stay out of the way of the walls, as they'd be less aware of what might happen next. The direct relationship between the audience and the object is now ambiguous and obscure.

My background is in sculpture, so making things with my hands is a very important part of my art practice. Using Physical Computing tools enables me to incorporate certain behaviour and sensors into objects through code, and is a chance to change the way I develop artwork. Hopefully, it throws up different issues and experiences for both myself and the audience.

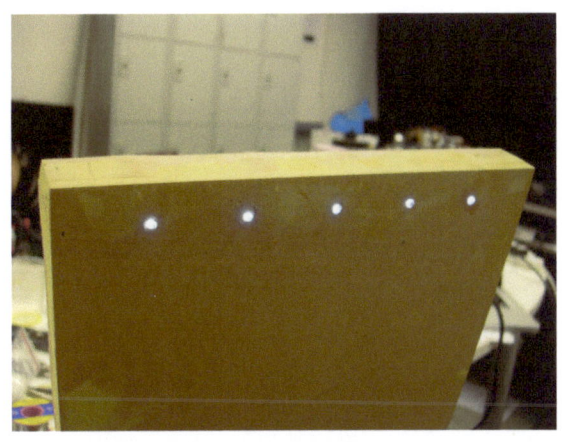

Sirius -

A Personal Heliostat

Samuel Price
Architect, Professional Media Practice

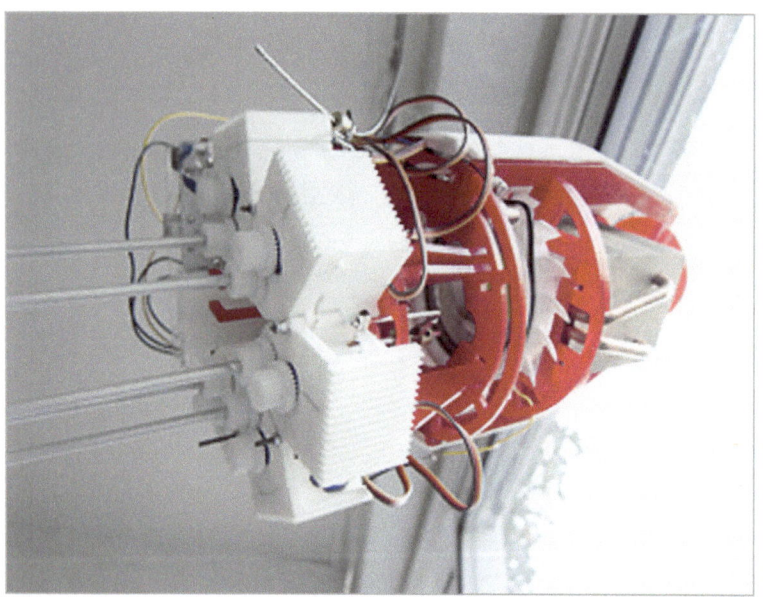

Laser-cut acrylic, 3D printed parts, servo motors, mirrors, Arduino microcontroller, light sensor.

The Personal Heliostat is a spatially aware actuator that seeks to reflect the illumination of sunlight into an internal space. Through mathematical computation, five mirrors act independently bisecting the suns path to throw light in user defined areas.

At night, *Sirius* switches to an internal LED that uses the same mirrors to create task lighting or diffuse illumination.

Physically building Sirius turned out to be far more demanding in time and technical know-how than originally anticipated. Even with limited Digital Prototyping studies, the final model required a lot of adjustment and workarounds.

The very definition of Physical Computing is a vast and fascinating pursuit. Sirius embraces this by striving to interpret our analogue world through digital and physical constructs.

Twitter Mood Flower

Zahir Abdi, BSc Computer Science
Mats Oftedal, BSc Computer Science
www.zahirabdi.co.uk

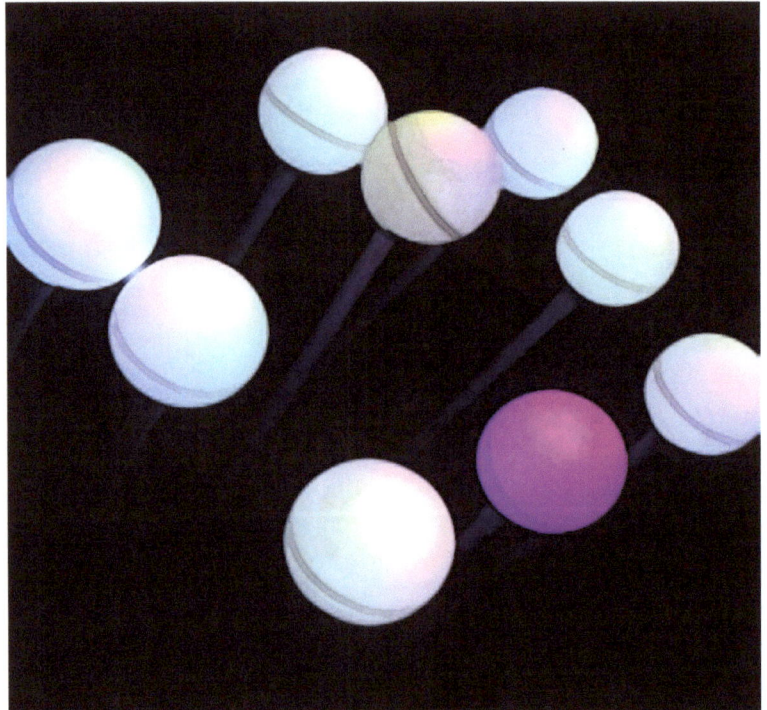

Arduino microcontroller, wireless networking module, liquid crystal display, touch-sensitive panel, potentiometers, fibreboard, tri-colour LEDs, plastic rods, ping pong balls.

The *Twitter Mood Flower* allows users to send tweets to Twitter based on their mood, and to recieve tweets. A set of predefined potentiometers have settings for mood and settings for level of mood which can be used to set the mood of tweet to be sent. When a tweet is recieved, the user flicks the middle rod containing RGB LEDs, which will display the tweet on the LCD screen.

Key challenges we faced included getting the Wifi to work and issues with the shift registers. We learnt alot about the physical aspect of computing and how certain components we have used are also used within the real world.

The interesting thing about Physical Computing is the way in that it can change ways of doing everyday activities. The *Twitter Mood Flower* is a fun interactive way of sending and recieving tweets based on physical interaction rather than sending plain text based tweets from a mobile or laptop.

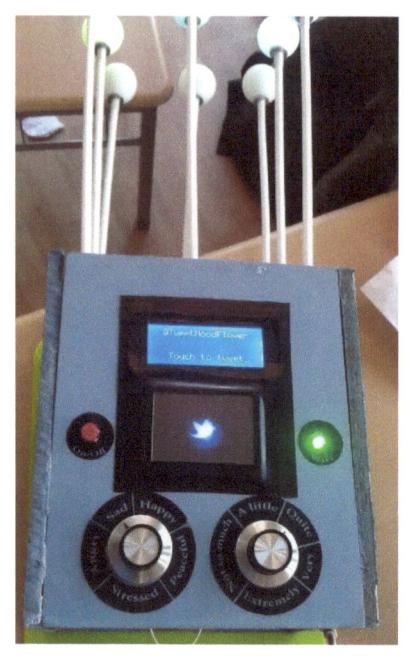

Remote Monitoring Deterrent

Nicola Blackwell, BSc Computer Science

Arduino microcontroller, wireless networking module, camera, temperature sensor, water pump, alarm.

This system was designed to deter animals from consuming garden flowers and vegetables, as this is something that had started to become a persistent issue for me.

Early one morning I saw rabbits playing outside, but on closer inspection they were also having breakfast, that being my flowers. This I thought was bad enough, when two pheasants came to join them.

I moved them on and checked the damage but unfortunately it was too late to save the plants. I planted new marigolds and watched all through the following week to see if the animals would do the same and they did. I needed to find a way of protecting my flowers without harming the animals, whilst making it clear that my plants were off the menu. The remote monitoring and deterring station was my solution to the problem.

The station is situated in a remote location. It monitors movement using a pyroelectric sensor. Once movement has been

detected, a series of deterrents are activated. A snapshot is automatically taken with a built-in IP camera and sent to a server using FTP. The temperature is recorded, while simultaneously an LED blinks and an audible alert warns of a forthcoming water jet activation. The water jet sprays continuously until movement is no longer detected. The built in water system is replenished with recycled rainwater.

The project provided many theoretical and technical challenges. The most prominent were power management and wireless Internet connection for the project due to its remote location.

Physical Computing is a very rewarding area of work and it can be used by people of almost any ability. Fantastic projects can be achieved using almost any component imaginable, enabling ideas to become a reality for very low cost.

My *Remote Monitoring Deterrent* has used as many recyclable materials as possible and components found in household appliances and motor vehicles. It has scope for alteration and expansion and provides ideas for further projects.

relational

liminal

luminous

Lost Trees

Steph Horak, MFA Computational Studio Arts

Arduino microcontroller, force-sensitive resistors, MAX/MSP.

Loosely based on the work of Ryan Jordan, *Lost Trees* is a Sensory Response System which creates a physical interface for live audio-visual performance. Singing with Light Dependent Resistors in the mouth and on the wrist, and manipulating two Force Sensitive Resistors with the hands, the data from these sensors is streamed into MaxMSP using Arduino as an interface. The Max patch channels this data through a series of audio transformations affecting the live vocals, and multiple cross-fade/distortion effects manipulate the custom-made projected visuals. The system is housed in a belt worn around the waist.

The key challenge was designing a Max patch interface that can be manipulated easily by others. My DIY-core/chaos approach suits me but would not lend itself to open source usage! The conceptual bias of this piece derives from a large-scale project which considers the possibility of 'afforestation' as an artistic output through community art projects.

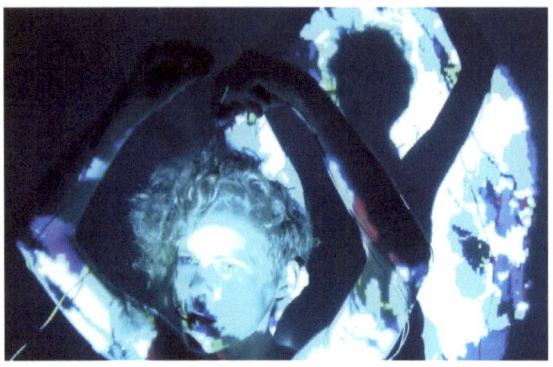

Physical Computing in the context of live audio-visual performance is very appealing and has a great deal of potential. Artists can design systems that sonify and visualize data streams manipulated using intuitive gestures that suit the artist. This allows for a much broader range of effects and choreographic styles that allow the artist to move beyond the constraints of the laptop screen.

Note: The MaxMSP patch was custom-designed and used the Arduino to Max code by Daniel Jolliffe based on a sketch by Thomas Ouellet Fredericks.

Too Much Punch

Una McDermott, MA Computational Arts

Arduino microcontroller, passive infrared sensor, solid state relay, light bulbs.

Too Much Punch is part performance, part video. My motivations are to deal with "real" space and time, and to reappropriate a recognisable object, creating a sense of fantasy, a new role for the skin of an object. The work consists of a makeup mirror comprising sixteen 11W bulbs, operated by an Arduino microcontroller through a solid state relay. A passive infrared sensor (PIR) detects movement of the observer. All bulbs illuminate together for a predetermined time and then the lights extinguish until further movement is detected. There were several challenges in this project, particularly working with alternating current and limiting the area of infrared detection and sensitivity.

Physical Computing supports playing with ideas, and easily realising the possibilities of working with an 'input' that yields an immediate response. This project was an example of how you can take an everyday object and add your own innovations to it to create something new and interesting.

Mood Cube

Katherine Eckford,
Siobhan McKenzie,
Natasha Potgieter
BA Computing and InteractionDesign

Arduino microcontroller, light-dependent resistors, LEDs, audio file
playback card.

The Mood Cube is an interactive light box. Three of the sides change colour when a hand hovers over them, shifting internal colours from blue, to red and to orange. When the box is reset, the colour is white. The back face has a pushbutton, which causes music from popular television programmes to be played. The box also incorporates a tilt switch, so that when the box is tipped it will turn on and off. Each side of the box has famous quotes cut out of it to add quirkiness to the design, and to inviting people to touch it. Each quote is associated with the name of the face of the mood cube that it is on. For example, the Zakk Wylde quote, "*I'm just worried that there's enough beer on the bus. That's the top priority at all times.*" is laser cut into the top of the box. Overall, we are happy with our design, it could be used for fun just to interact with, for kids, or as an art object.

Morpheus

Fabio Lattanzi Antinori,
MFA Computational Studio Arts

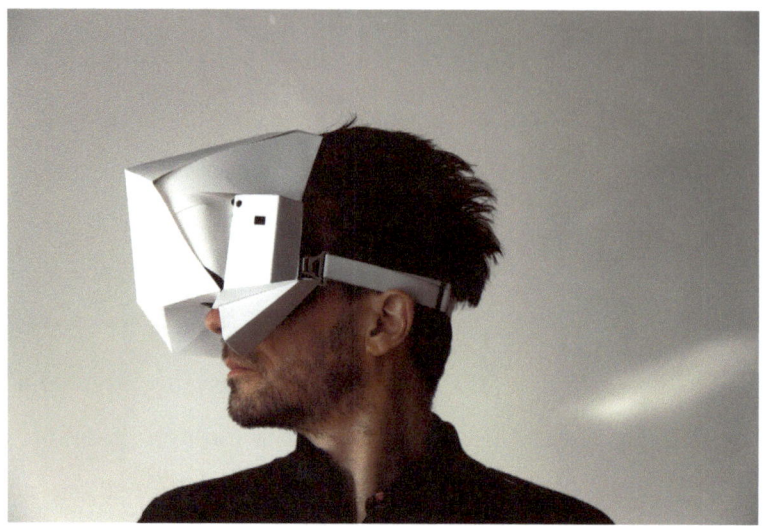

Arduino microcontroller, LEDs, infrared distance sensors, folded styrene.

I am interested in using Physical Computing technology to realise wearable artwork, which allows people to experience altered states of sensorial perception and explore new perspectives on everyday life.

This project creates a platform for people to live their dreams, no matter how wild they can be, while sleeping. Lucid dreaming is the phenomenon of having a dream and being aware of it; it is often experienced by accident or it may occur as the result of years of training. By finding an open passage between the two layers of consciousness and unconsciousness, people can learn how to direct their dreams and experience an existence outside the physical limits of day-to-day life, exploring the magic liminal zone in between reality and fantasy.

The idea behind *Morpheus* originates from the theories of J. Campbell and C.G. Jung, who believed that dreams could help us grow and resolve our emotional issues by connecting us to the collective unconscious through the use of symbols.

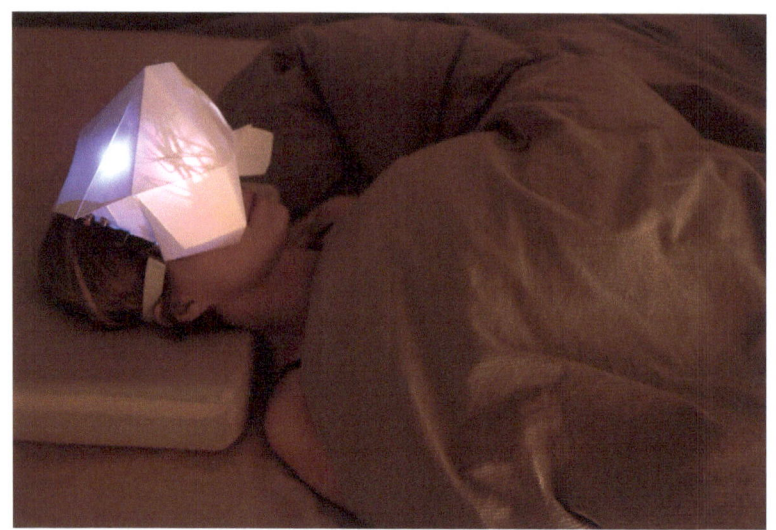

From this point of view dreams are as important to mankind as myths and fairytales. According to Jung, living a myth would help people to reconcile themselves with the 'shadow component' of their being, and in doing so, allow them to be complete.

As an artwork, *Morpheus* is meant to represent an experience whose narrative is left open and about which the interpretation is to be made by the participant.

The project aims to explore the territory in between science and spirituality, knowledge and beliefs.

Overall I am very happy with *Morpheus*, but I somewhat feel that this is the beginning, rather than a conclusion, as there are many parts which I need to explore better. One of the future scenarios I envisaginge with particular enthusiasm is sharing data online among different people using different masks; when a REM phase is detected, data will be sent over the net to trigger the LED lights of another mask, and so on. This way we could imagine a network of people who influence each other while dreaming, potentially exploring possibilities of joint/shared lucid dreaming. Events could be staged in galleries or theatres etc where people would go to sleep and share their lucid dreams.

Special thanks to: Alicja Pytlewska from the Royal College of Art in London for her help and support.

During the making of this project:

3 IR emitters were burned

4 IR collectors didn't work in the end

1 soldering iron went missing somewhere

1 soldering iron stopped working

1 now works like a killer, but I still don't know how to replace its bit

1 Honeywell HOA1405 never worked from the start but I only found out at the very end. Lots of jumpwires and cables were sacrificed or just went missing

4 sheets of styrene were used

A big roll of Fabriano white smooth paper 320gsm was put to good use

I have become good friend of the staff at Maplin Liverpool street and 4D Model Shop

I have learned that unless you buy a student card you won't have a student card

The smell of solder can bring you back to childhood but overall, it isn't a good thing, no!

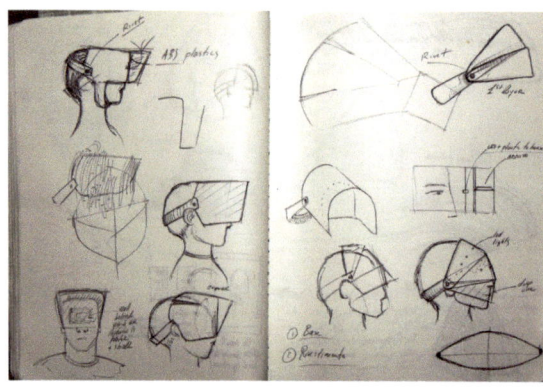

Brock Craft, PhD FRSA

Brock is a creative technologist and Lecturer in Arts Computing at Goldsmiths, Department of Computing and a Research Fellow at the Institute of Education, London Knowledge Lab.

He has been playing with interactivity ever ever since crashing his first cardboard-box-and-LED spaceship as a kid, in the 70s.

He is fascinated by obsolete display technologies, especially nixie tubes, split-flap displays, edge-lit readouts, and flip-dot signs.

Eleanor Dare, PhD

Eleanor is a fine artist and Lecturer in Arts Computing at Goldsmiths, Department of Computing.

Her first experience with DIY electricity involved being thrown across a room by an old television set.

Since that incident she has stuck to working with very low voltages.

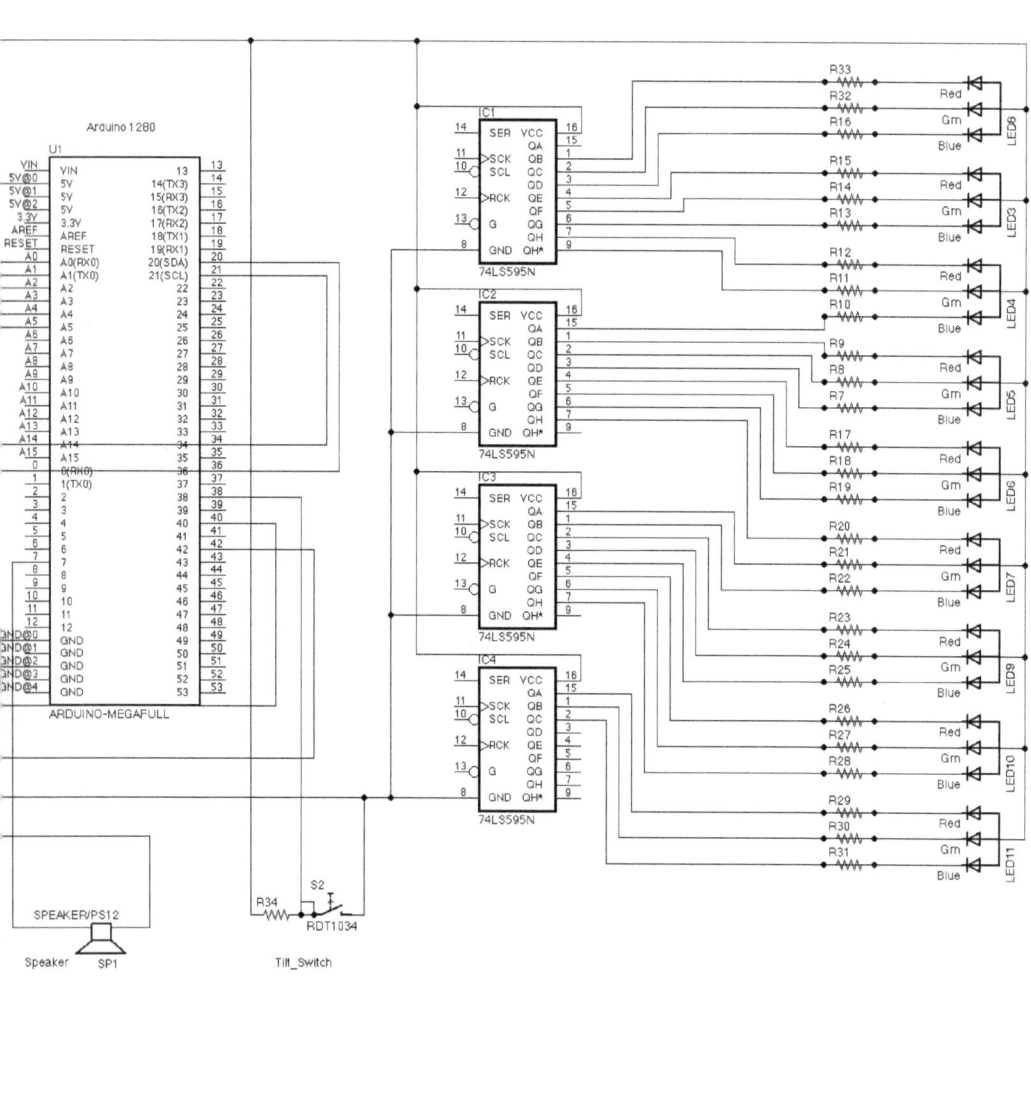

www.ingramcontent.com/pod-product-compliance
Lightning Source LLC
Chambersburg PA
CBHW041101180526
45172CB00001B/52